Live Every Moment

My Life as A Super Extra Ordinary Mom

Live Every Moment

My Life as A Super Extra Ordinary Mom

by Shatanese Reese
© 2018

Copyright © 2018
by Shatanese Reese

All rights reserved. No part of this book may be reprinted or reproduced in any form or by any electronic, mechanical, or other means, now known or hereafter invented, including photocopy, recording, and information storage and retrieval, without permission in writing from the publisher.

ISBN: 978-0-9996746-0-4
Library of Congress Control Number: 2018962139

Designed and Published by:
The Solid Foundation Group, LLC
www.TheSolidFoundationGroup.com

Printed in the United States of America

DEDICATIONS

To my grandma, Edna Mae. Thank you for being you.
You are greatly missed.

ACKNOWLEDGEMENTS

Heavenly Father, thank you for your grace, love and mercy on my life. Thank you for pursuing me even at my lowest points and for loving me when I did not love myself. Thank you for placing the desire to write a book on my heart.

Thank you to ALL my family and friends who have encouraged me on this journey called life, especially my Mom, Mary K, who is the epitome of perseverance. Marcée & Tara, may our love of books and reading be exemplified through this project. Thank you both for your editing efforts, truly a labor of love. #3musketeersforever.

Dethra, Deborah, Tangie and Monica, you may never fully know the impact you have had on my life. Thank you for encouraging me to keep going and to not give up on this project. Meleila, Stacy and Sonja, thank you for always being willing to pray for me at the drop of a hat, no matter the time of day.

To my children, this legacy is for you. My husband, Steve, my best friend. Thank you for being right there by my side, encouraging me, telling me the things that needed to be said that I didn't want to hear at times and for always loving me and pushing me to keep going.

Cutina - I finally did it!

TABLE OF CONTENTS

	Introduction	1
Chapter 1:	Thoughts to Run From	7
Chapter 2:	Dear Trusted Adult	15
Chapter 3:	Redefining Loss	19
Chapter 4:	The Making of a Veterinarian	23
Chapter 5:	My Son, The Marine	27
Chapter 6:	No Bullying Allowed	33
Chapter 7:	May I Help You?	37
Chapter 8:	Her Name is Nina Sophia	43
Chapter 9:	Our Miracle Baby	53
Chapter 10:	Prayers for Our Children	61
Chapter 11:	They Said I Have Cancer	95
Chapter 12:	Keeping It All Together	105
Chapter 13:	Chuckles for the Soul	113

INTRODUCTION

In the Beginning:
Coming Out of the Darkness

"The purpose behind the suffering you are going through is to kick you into a new freedom from false definitions of who you are."

Said by Paul Zaul to Billy Graham's grandson, Tullian Tchividjian.

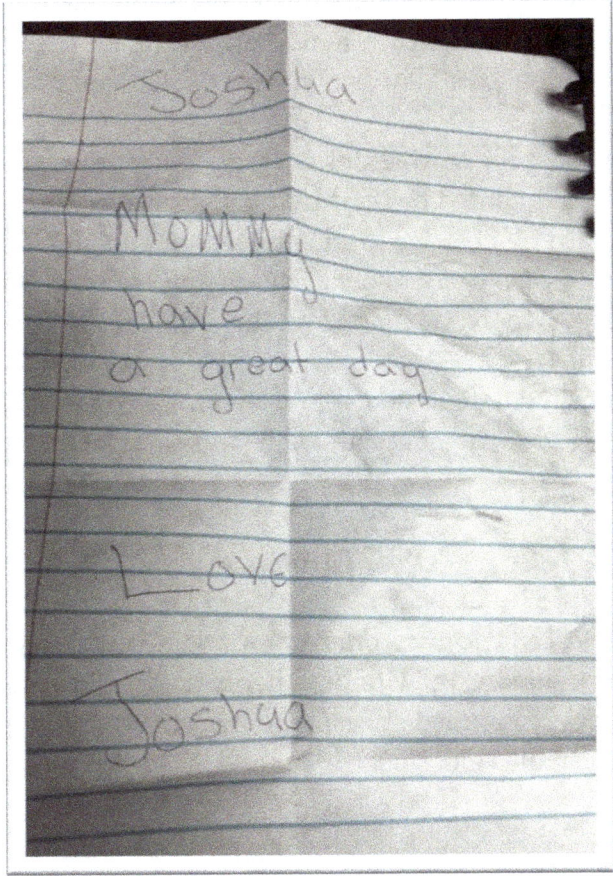

At times, I am still shocked that I am the mother of six children. There have been moments when I count them all just to make certain I am not dreaming. Often, people I encounter are also shocked that I have six children. I always reply, "Yep! and I have the birthing stories to prove it!"

By the time this book is published I will have been a mother for over twenty years. The late nights and early mornings, boo-boos which required band-aids, bedtime books read, lunches made with sweet notes attached... those are the tasks and events that define my experience as a mother. The image of the note from my son makes it all worthwhile.

My purpose for writing this book is to encourage anyone who has been haunted by their past and struggles to break free from old patterns. I strive to encourage that person, through my experiences as a parent, to believe in themselves and offer insight. God is there, no matter what.

To truly understand and appreciate my experience as a mother, you have to understand a little about my childhood, my past.

Once Upon a Time...

There was a little girl from Iowa who did not know her worth. Her relationship with both her biological father and stepfather were strained at best. She was left attempting to fill an unquenchable void.

Throughout her primary and secondary school years, she sought acknowledgement, love and affection from those who were either not interested, not available or simply unable to give her what she so desperately sought. This trend carried on through her post-secondary experiences. She eventually married but yet the insatiable void remained. That little girl was me. I look back in my mind's eye at that little girl and I want to hold her and shower her with love. I want to tell her that she is just enough. If I could go back in time, I would grab that little girl and take her out of her circumstances, running with her and never looking back.

In the beginning of my adulthood there was a shroud of darkness that hovered over me. Negative thoughts of my past threatened to hold me down as if I was shackled. The thoughts were heavy...very heavy and often too difficult to carry on a regular basis. In my mind, I would think of other places to be, my thoughts often went to:

Flowers everywhere...blowing in the wind.
Reds, purples and yellows. White snow...untouched. Glistening in the moonlight. Sparkling. No footprints. Crunch of the footsteps. Which way?
The right, the left, forward, backward? Which way?
Walking, running. Standing still.

I would have frequent conversations with God: "Lord, where are you? I do not sense your presence. I do not see you in my life. I feel very alone and without guidance.

Am I worth your time? Am I worth your love? Am I worth your acceptance? Do I have to walk a certain way? Do I have to talk in a certain manner? Do I have to have a certain education level? Tell me! What is the secret to being totally accepted?"

One could say I was lost. In order to be found however, you have to know where you are. I did not know. It is important to note that I did in fact know of God. I understood that He existed but I did not have a true relationship with Him. I did not know that He was willing to meet me right where I was.

I want each person to see that He loves them exactly as they are even if they never change. I want them to embrace the possibility of change. Embrace the possibility of a better future. Embrace the possibility of truly benefiting from their past. And benefiting from those experiences that threatened to drain each person of their very existence and will power.

The Light at the End Of The Tunnel...

I still remember the experience as if it occurred yesterday. I decided to retreat from the world. I needed to go somewhere to hear myself think. To know who I was at that moment and to figure out who I wanted to be. I stumbled across Ignatius House and booked my spot. The property was beautiful, peaceful. I could immediately sense God's presence as soon as I stepped out of my vehicle. The serenity was evident and peace was abounding. I walked towards an area of the property which overlooked the Chattahoochee River. I could hear the leaves crunching under foot as I slowly made my way to the deck.

I could see the river gradually, calmly making its way past the weathered banks. As I leaned on the deck rail, I inhaled deeply and then exhaled s l o w l y. I could hear the birds chirping as they made their way up to the tops of the trees. Looking up at the trees watching them gently swaying in the fall breeze, as if they were smiling and waving at me. It was then that I heard His voice,

"I accept you. Right where you are."

As the tears slowly rolled down my cheeks, I smiled and sighed in relief. The love and acceptance I had been seeking was there the entire time. I felt like Dorothy when she discovered she had the power to go home all along, but that she needed to learn a few lessons first.

Like Dorothy, I learned about the limits of friends (the scarecrow), belief in myself (the cowardly lion) and the value of flexibility (the tin man). Tears still threaten to fall just thinking about His love and acceptance in that moment.

Accept yourself and understand where you are. Self-acceptance is empowering. Self-love is freeing. Self-awareness is the key to living a full life. I pray this book offers inspiration on my own journey of loving myself, understanding who I am in Christ and the beauty of self-acceptance.

SHATANESE REESE

CHAPTER ONE
Thoughts to Run From

Negative self-talk can be debilitating. I struggled with negative self-talk for a long period of time in my life. It is draining and unproductive. It can be similar to weights that have been placed on every limb. I've learned that I cannot escape negative thoughts, they creep up in my conscious freely:

Negative thoughts...wanting to run and not look back.
Running from the negative thoughts.
Pushing past my fears.
Pushing past the voices that are saying...

You're too thin.
You're not big enough.
Your breasts - not big enough.
Your stomach - not flat enough.
Your butt - too flat.
Your hair - lacks style.
Your clothes - too boring.

Your everything - not enough.
They like her better than you.
She's smarter than you are.
He'd have more fun with someone else.
They prefer a different mom.
You suck as a mom.
You're not as good as you think you are.

Running from the negative thoughts.
How can I break free? What do I need to do?

What is the point?

I hate who I have become. Someone who is riddled with self-doubt and insecurities. How do I help my children fight insecurities? How does anyone fight insecurities?

They cover me.
They envelope me.
They fight to squelch my breath.

I cannot breathe.
I feel heavy. The burden is too heavy.
Will I ever be enough?

No.

How?

Stop it. STOP IT.

*STOOOOOOOOOOOOOOOOPPPPPPP
IIIIIIIIIIIITTTTTTTTTT!*

Recoiling into a fetal position. Not wanting to look out. You don't see me. I don't see you.

Run...fly...drag...fall...heavy.

Lifeless.

*Where is the sun?
Where is the Son?
Where?*

*Is it in here?
Is He in here?
Who is in here?*

*Not me.
Not her.
Not that person.
Yes, that person.*

*I am trying to swim...something is grabbing my arm.
Something is grabbing my leg. What is it?
What could it be? It is grabbing my neck.*

*It is the past...The dark, ugly past.
Threatening to pull me down into an abyss.
I fight...I kick...I writhe...I scream.*

Help!

Stop! Now! Swallowing water. Swallowing death...
I can't.
What is love? Do I love me? Can I love me?
Am I lovable?

There is fire...it is dull.
The sum total of my life.

Achieving...trying to succeed.
Attempting to reach an unattainable goal.

It is too high. Out of reach.
Running. Perfection. Imperfection.
I hate. I loathe. I detest. I despise.

Disgust.
Anger.
Frustration.
Hurt.
Pain.

Cry...cry...cry....
He loves me. He loves me not. He loves me.
H e l o v e s m e...n.

When?

I want to be free. I want to shine.
I want to be ok in my own skin.

Why?

Tears...crying...cleansing...exploding.
Screaming. Shouting.
Running. Fighting. Jumping.
Bleeding...hurting...still hurting.
Healing sometimes...hurting me.
Hurting others.

H U R T.
Hiding Under Rough Times.

No. Not. Never. Maybe. Possibly.

Yesterday. Today. Tomorrow.
Forever. Eternity. Infinity.
Infertility. Indefinitely. Infidelity.

Future.
Growth hurts.
Pain.
Forgiven. Grace. Mercy.
Never mind.

I tried. We tried. They tried.
They cried.

Reality equals perception equals deception equals anxiety.
What is truth?
Actions equal truth.
Actions equal truth.

I have it all. I have never. I have always. I have. I have.
What next?

Me. You. Us. Them. Him.

I would be spent after these types of tirades in my head. I had to find solace and peace. After tirelessly fighting with the onslaught of thoughts, one of my favorite scriptures on which I meditate during times of despair is Philippians 4:8...

> "Finally, brethren, whatsoever things are true, whatsoever things are honorable, whatsoever things are just, whatsoever things are pure, whatsoever things are lovely, whatsoever things are of good report; if there be any virtue, and if there be any praise, think on these things."

I was that person. The person who did not know her true worth and identity.

> *Break free...break out...get out...you are free.*
> *You can do it.*
> *Do not stop. Keep fighting for yourself.*
> *For your true self.*
> *Who are you?*
> *Who do you want to be? God made you.*
> *You are here now.*

The online dictionary states the definition of acceptance is, "The action or process of being received as adequate or suitable, typically to be admitted into a group."

The definition of self-worth is, "Confidence in one's own worth or abilities; self-respect."

I am confident. You cannot take that from me. I know my worth. I know my abilities. When was the last time you took a moment to assess your talents?

Look inwardly to understand your own worth. Meditate on each talent. This is how you manifest unconditional love for self. Everyone deserves to feel this sort of self-love.

The seeds of mistrust breed in the fertile ground of abuse, hurt and misunderstanding. Germinated by secrecy and the rays of opportunity, mixed with self-gratification.

Have you ever believed you were worth it?

Lie on the floor, with arms outstretched. Ask God to come in. Invite Him in. Ask Him to show you a glimpse of true love. Ask Him to make it real for you. Ask Him to increase your confidence and understanding of your self-worth.

The failed relationships almost drained me. The relationship, or lack thereof, with my fathers, almost drained me. The relationship with my childhood almost drained me. My need for affirmation almost drained me. Infidelity almost drained me. Financial fear almost drained me. Comparison almost drained me. Miscarriages almost drained me. Career management almost drained me. Cancer almost killed me.

But God...and His grace and mercy!

The Truth and The Beginning of Revelation...
These are scriptures that remind me of my worth.

Be Still and Know That I Am God. Psalm 46:10

God's ever presence is all power. He appears in the everyday small activities of life. Even those horrible moments when all we want to do is crawl into the bed like a dejected ball and shut out the world, God is in those moments.

For I know the plans I have for you, plans to prosper you and not to harm you. Jeremiah 29:11

God's plan for our lives is unstoppable. There may be detours but ultimately, God's plan will prevail. There is just one condition, we must listen.

Lean not to your own understanding. Proverbs 3:5

It is easy to attempt to understand the world through our own lens and experiences. The God factor kicks in and we have to view people through God's lens as well as view our circumstances through God's lens.

CHAPTER TWO
Dear Trusted Adult – I Am Free!

We know that in all things God works for the good of those who love him, who have been called according to his purpose. Romans 8:28

My past often impacted my ability to be an effective parent. One incident in particular dealt with the sexual abuse I suffered at the hand of a trusted adult. I decided to change my trajectory and write a letter to the perpetrator, the person who stole my innocence but not my future. I finally decided to free myself from that prison of shame, disappointment and sadness.

Dear Trusted Adult,

Today is the day that I let it all go.

Today is the day that I release the shame that has been prevalent in my life as a result of the choices you made nearly 30 years ago.

I am releasing the shame which has been like a large immovable anchor tethered to a small balloon, weighing it down, never allowing it to take flight and float freely.

I release the shame that has at times washed over me like crashing waves on a stormy beach, causing me to feel as if I was drowning, unable to breathe.

Today is the day I no longer look at all males suspiciously as they interact with my children. I will no longer stand on the sideline questioning their motivation and expressions of love. Don't get me wrong, I will continue to be discerning but I will no longer project my own limiting fears onto my children.

I will no longer be afraid of the bumps in the night and the shadows that cast their faint, dark images into my bedroom. Today is the day that I release it all. I let go of the thoughts in my head which told me I was not worth fighting for. The thoughts that told me I was not worth protecting. The thoughts that told me I was not worth saving and that I was never enough. I release them. I release the feelings of being tainted, damaged and used, no longer pure.

Today, I forgive myself for all of my past failed relationships and my attempts to find love in all the wrong places. Today, many years later as an adult, is the day that I give myself, without hesitation, to my children.

I will surrender to their frequent requests for hugs, tickle time, and innocent touches which have until today, threatened to evoke distant yet uncomfortable memories. I will fight against triggers and flashbacks and choose to live in the present.

Effective today, I will willingly give in to their earnest yearnings for a mother's love, genuine love from a trusted adult.

Today is the day that I tell that beautiful little girl in the past that it is OK to come out of her protective space and to accept the love from those around her. Today is the day that I tell her she is unique, special, and important.

Today is the day that I embrace her, caress her head, and tell her that she can relax because she is safe.

Dear Trusted Adult, today is the day that I forgive you. This letter is a gift as it marks the day that I release you. You were a trusted adult, someone who was entrusted to care for me. I realize now the flaw was in you and not in me.

In all honesty, this letter is a gift to myself because today is the day I am finally free.

CHAPTER THREE
Redefining Loss

Becoming a mother was not always an easy feat. There were some moments that left me questioning my very existence.

"I am sorry, Mrs. Reese. The pregnancy is no longer viable."

Tears welled up in my eyes as the doctor continued with the final details of the visit. I could not hear much of what was being said as I focused on the sense of loss I felt. My body felt heavy and my spirit was grieved.

The appointment eventually concluded and I made my way to the elevator. The doors closed and finally, I was alone. Alone with my thoughts, fears, disappointments, and sadness. I became painfully aware that I was physically alone as well. The small being who had been growing inside of me for the past several weeks was no longer there.

Gone…never to be held in my arms.

Suddenly, the elevator door opened and in walked a very pregnant woman. I quickly looked at the floor, fighting back fresh tears. As I exited the elevator, I could no longer hold back the flood of tears that had been threatening to overtake me. With my vision blurred, I clumsily made my way to my car and slid in behind the steering wheel. I buried my face in my hands and let the tears flow freely, filling the car with the sounds of my weeping.

Anger entered my consciousness. Why God? Why? What had I done to warrant this experience? What had caused my body to reject the life that had been allowed to begin? Why? Do you not love me?

The sense of emptiness I felt continued to grow and the weight of my grief became heavier, unbearable. I decided to make my way home.

I am not certain how I drove the distance to our house as I do not remember the trip at all. Once I entered our home, I left everything I had in my hands by the door and slipped off my shoes. The top of the stairs appeared far off in the distance but I knew my solace was near. I slowly climbed the stairs to our bedroom, dragging my feet the entire way. I finally reached the landing, walked into our room and crawled into our bed, fully clothed. I curled into a ball and attempted to shut out the world as well as the emotional and physical pain I was now fully feeling.

I have experienced a total of four miscarriages in my life, each heavy-laden with its own process of grief. I say they are my four Angel Babies. Many might say that a miscarriage during the first trimester is not as devastating as one during a later trimester or even after birth. I say that a loss is a loss.

I believe there are two processes that occur during such a loss: the physical healing of the body and the emotional healing of the mind. Will it happen again? What can I do to avoid it? Should we even try again? I suppose one could also include the healing of the spirit, a sort of reconciliation with God.

I have had numerous conversations with God, at various stages of my pregnancies. After the second miscarriage, there were times shortly after learning I was expecting when I would pray fervently prior to taking a trip to the restroom.

"Lord, please do not let me see anything on this toilet paper after I wipe. Please, Lord. Please."

"Lord, please make this cramping feeling go away as I do not know if I can handle another loss."

Anger-focused questions also bounced around in my head. "Father, if it is not your will for me to carry this child full-term, then why did you allow me to become pregnant in the first place?"

Ultimately, I found verses in the Bible for focus and told myself that God knows best. Some might wonder why I would allow myself to become pregnant again and again...and again.

I firmly believed God had a plan for my life and for the pain I had experienced with each loss. I believed, and still believe, that I was not being punished for some past sin. I imagine that some day when I am in heaven, I will hear four voices which will say,

"Hi Mommy. We've missed you."

Until that day, I choose to focus on healing and the blessings I presently have in my life. You too can choose to focus on healing and redefine what loss means to you.

CHAPTER FOUR
The Making of a Veterinarian

I always knew the day would come where I would have to say good-bye. I just did not realize how difficult it would be. While traveling to take my oldest daughter to Iowa for college, I received the news that I had cancer in multiple areas within my breasts. Days prior I had been informed that I had breast cancer in one breast and after additional testing I was now being told I was facing a double mastectomy. There I was in one of the busiest airports in the world, on the phone with the doctor fighting back tears. I did not want to mar my daughter's experience of heading to college so I kept it together as best as I could.

We had a beautiful time exploring her new home away from home. We shopped, unpacked, ate, organized and walked the campus. Experiencing her new world through her eyes was awesome. It was exhilarating allowing her to find her own stride.

"Watch over her God," is what I prayed consistently. I was thankful for the professional campus relationships I had forged nearly 20 years before, almost as if in anticipation of this moment.

For the past 18 years I have seen her daily, talked to, laughed with, wiped tears, watched her grow, face challenges, explore, excel, deal with disappointment, and just BE.

We went to the last activity before my departure and I could feel the lump growing in my throat.

"Well I've got to get to the airport, Sweet Pea. I love you and will text you when I arrive."

"Love you, Mom. Thanks for helping me get settled."

As I drove away, I watched her disappear into the building and the tears I had been holding back from reflecting on her future away from home and processing the call I had received earlier about my cancer diagnosis, flowed with great force. I could barely see the road!! I brushed away the tears as quickly as they fell.

Yes, I knew she was going to be just fine. Yes, she has a good head on her shoulders. But still, she is my first baby.

As I was depressing the gas pedal to quickly traverse the 30 miles between the cities to catch my flight, our song suddenly came on the radio. All of the feelings that had been percolating came flooding once again to the surface like a tidal wave crashing against the rocks on a beach.

"I'm falling so I'm taking my time on my ride." A fresh new set of tears began to fall.

"I've been thinking too much (help me)" the radio belted out.

I finally turned the volume up loudly and bobbed my head in sync with the music. I knew she was going to take her time on her college ride and I knew I was going to face cancer one day at a time.

As your children grow older, you too will face a day where they will turn and walk into their destiny. You can face this moment with bravery as you reflect on the foundation you have established for them and the hope they will call you whenever the need arises.

CHAPTER FIVE
My Son, The Marine - The Few. The Proud.

That moment when you are riding with your teen-aged son and you use BOTH feet to push down on your imaginary passenger-side brakes because he's approaching a traffic light too quickly!

My son, Azaan, left the comfort of our home to travel to Parris Island, South Carolina. This was not a vacation adventure. No, the trip was for basic training to become a Marine. I fully supported his decision to serve our country and knew for several months that the day would come. So, why did I have a lump in my throat and feel churning in the pit of my stomach?

Not long before his departure, I was listening to National Public Radio (NPR) and the featured story of the hour was the involvement of the United States Marines Corps in World War I. The Battle of Belleau Wood was cited as "one of the bloodiest and most ferocious battles the United States Armed Forces would fight in the war."

This historic battle, which occurred near the Marne River in France, is where our soldiers received the nickname, "Devil Dogs." This term of endearment was a result of the soldiers' diligence, ferociousness, sacrifice and valor exhibited during the battle.

To hear or read the full **Morning Edition: NPR, France to Honor, 'Les Sammies,' Uncle Sam's World War I Troops** story, visit:

https://www.npr.org/2017/06/30/534980339/france-to-honor-les-sammies-uncle-sam-s-world-war-i-trooops

As I listened to the gory details of the battle, it hit me. All of the emotions I had been loosely managing up until that moment bubbled quickly to the surface. The realization that my oldest son would soon be training to possibly fight in future similar battles came crashing over me like a giant wave thrashing on rocks near a shore.

Fighting back tears, I wondered how I would cope. How was I going to release my son to the United States Government and simply trust that he was going to be okay? I came up with a few ways to cope.

Be Present

As the days passed with fierce quickness, I was intentional about the time I spent with my son. I knew in advance that he would be without his cell phone during basic training, and he would not be allowed to write for the first 2-3 weeks. No immediate contact? Wow. (Breathe, mom, breathe.) This reality pushed me to soak up as much of his presence as I could while he was still at home. I took in every detail I saw; his smile, his laugh, his quirkiness and his positive, brave attitude.

I hugged him a little tighter and listened a little more intently. I was being present.

Focus on the Positives

It would have been easier to focus on the state of our governmental affairs at the time and the possibility of war. I had to be intentional about thinking on other aspects. There was no doubt in my mind that my son was going to change tremendously as a result of this new chapter in his life. I focused on the positive changes. I focused on the great life lessons he was going to learn, the people he would eventually meet and the level of maturity he was going to gain as a result of basic training and beyond. He had aspirations to make the Marines his career. I focused on the successful career he was going to definitely have.

Pray

I did not underestimate the power of prayer. I prayed for my son's experience at basic training and continued to pray once he began his tours. Specifically, I prayed Psalm 91 over him and included his name within the verses to personalize the scripture and make it come alive.

Psalm 91

*1 Whoever dwells in the shelter of the Most High
will rest in the shadow of the Almighty.
2 Azaan will say of the Lord, "He is my refuge
and my fortress, my God, in whom I will trust."
3 Surely he will save Azaan from the fowler's
snare and from the deadly pestilence.*

4 He will cover Azaan with his feathers, and under his wings Azaan will find refuge; his faithfulness will be Azaan's shield and rampart.
5 Azaan will not fear the terror of night, nor the arrow that flies by day,
6 nor the pestilence that stalks in the darkness, nor the plague that destroys at midday.
7 A thousand may fall at Azaan's side, ten thousand at Azaan's right hand, but it will not come near Azaan.
8 Azaan will only observe with his eyes and see the punishment of the wicked.
9 If Azaan says, "The Lord is my refuge," and you make the Most High your dwelling,
10 no harm will overtake Azaan, no disaster will come near Azaan's tent.
11 For he will command his angels concerning Azaan to guard Azaan in all his ways;
12 they will lift Azaan up in their hands, so that Azaan will not strike his foot against a stone.
13 Azaan will tread on the lion and the cobra; Azaan will trample the great lion and the serpent.
14 "Because Azaan loves me," says the Lord, "I will rescue him; I will protect Azaan, for he acknowledges my name.
15 Azaan will call on me, and I will answer him; I will be with Azaan in trouble, I will deliver Azaan and honor him.
16 With long life I will satisfy Azaan and show him my salvation."

In Jesus' name. Amen.

By being present, focusing on the positive, and praying, my son's departure became just a little bit more palatable. Try these tips for any loved one you may have who has chosen to serve in our military or may be facing a major move. The tips will allow you to truly enjoy and focus on what is most important, your relationship with your loved one.

CHAPTER SIX
No Bullying Allowed – Empowering His Voice

"Mommy, the kids in my class and on my bus say they think I am a girl and ask if I am gay."

I've had enough! Too many times my son has come to me with a downcast look, his shoulders slumped, and near tears after hearing an onslaught of taunts from his peers throughout the day.

The definitions of *bullying* range from, "abuse and mistreatment of someone vulnerable" to "unwanted, aggressive behavior among school aged children that involves a real or perceived power imbalance...the behavior is repeated, or has the potential to be repeated, over time." *Harassment* is defined as, "causing the person alarm or distress."

Teasing is defined as, "to laugh at and criticize someone in a way that is either friendly and playful, or cruel and unkind." Either of these definitions can apply to what my son is experiencing and I want it to stop.

I don't think our schools are equipped to handle this issue. At least not the school where our children currently attend. Why do I say this? Because the behavior continues to occur with no end in sight.

This is not a discussion about sexuality or gender identity. It is a discussion about my son feeling ostracized and targeted at a place where he spends the majority of his day. I don't like it.

My husband and I read each of the newsletters when they come home with our children and I do not see any workshops being offered that address bullying. The school offers themed weeks to deal with drug abuse, team spirit, and even future vocation choices, but not one on how to deal with a bully or the consequences of bullying. Our children even come home discussing the active shooter awareness sessions in which they have participated, but not once have I heard about discussions dealing with bullying.

I am tired of telling my son to ignore the comments and, "It's not what you are called but what you answer to." I am sure he too is tired of hearing, "Someone is always going to have something to say about you so you have to deal with it." Deal with it? How?

What am I to do as a parent? Our attempts to appeal to the school's administration on our son's behalf seem futile. Move him to another school? Will that truly guarantee that he will no longer experience taunting? Am I to home-school him until he reaches a certain age?

These choices all seem as if it is my son's fault for his experience. Or perhaps I should boycott the entire school system until the perpetrators are "brought to justice."

I know my son is not the first to have this type of experience nor will he be the last. This fact does not lessen the aggravation, disappointment, and sheer sadness I feel each time I hear my son recount his day at school.

A recent report shared on dosomething.org states that over 3.2 million students are victims of bullying each year. There are equally stark statistics regarding how many teens attempt to take their lives due to bullying. Unaddressed bullying manifests itself in terrible and ugly ways, even into adulthood.

Please hear my son's voice...

> *"I don't appreciate you calling me those names. It feels disrespectful and hurtful. In the Bible it says to treat others as you want to be treated. Would you say mean things to your mom?"*

Something has to change. You are definitely your children's advocate. Typically, they do not have a voice and parents must be their voices. If your child is facing a challenge, I encourage you to stand firm and empower their voice.

CHAPTER SEVEN
May I Help You? - Hannah J.

Hannah: "Mommy?"

Me: "I'm using the restroom." Which typically means, "Give me a minute and I will be right with you."

She proceeds to come in and says, while pointing at her left side, "I have a scratch right here."

Please tell me in which language does, "I'm using the restroom" actually mean? "Come in!?!?"

We selected Hannah as her name due to Hannah in the Bible. In I Samuel 1, the Bible states, "the Lord had closed her womb" and she was unable to bear children until she was blessed to give birth to a son, Samuel.

I had experienced two losses before Hannah was conceived and therefore felt a connection with the character and believed the name was fitting. Hannah was our rainbow child.

Hannah Jolie (Hannah J.) was born on a chilly November day. She is our most attentive child. She anticipates the needs of others and responds quickly and earnestly which comes very easily and naturally to her.

I was on a healthy streak and was determined to cook something edifying for my body and for the rest of my family. I found a tofu recipe and decided to try it.

"May I help you?" Hannah J. asked.

"Yes, of course!" I said excitedly.

We worked together nicely. Hannah washed off ingredients while I chopped and shredded carrots, ginger, and green onions. With supervision, Hannah also volunteered to stir the ingredients, such as the peanut butter and tofu that had been combined in the pan.

"Mommy, this is going to be delicious!" Hannah said confidently.

We worked diligently to prepare a delicious, healthy alternative for our family. Our family LOVED it! I believe I have created a chef!

Wikipedia describes memory as, "Among its other roles, **memory** functions to guide present behavior and to predict future outcomes. **Memory** in **childhood** is qualitatively and quantitatively different from the **memories** formed and retrieved in late adolescence and the adult years."

I want to impact the memories upon which my children will draw in as many positive ways as possible. Research shows that positive memories are directly linked to positive emotions and positive thinking. An article appearing in the Harvard Health Publishing states "There is power in positive thinking. Positive emotions are linked with better health, longer life, and greater well-being."

Our time in the kitchen certainly brought back memories of watching my grandmother and aunt in the kitchen during the holidays and peering in on my mother as she prepared delicacies for dinner such as salmon croquettes. I am thankful for the gift of cooking that I can share with each of my children, especially Hannah. Hopefully, she will hold on to those moments as cherished memories to one-day pass on to her children. I encourage you to create as many special memories as possible with your loved ones. Their health depends on it!

CHAPTER EIGHT
Her Name is Nina Sophia

Her: "Mommy..."

Me: "Yes, Sweetheart?"

Her: "I'm not Sweetheart. I am Nina!"

I guess I'll get it through my thick head someday! 😂 The main reason I use sweetheart is so I don't run the risk of calling her the wrong name!

#LargeFamilyChronicles #MemoryGame #SixKids #NinaSophia #SheIsThatOne

Nina: Coughs open-mouthed at the dinner table.

Me: "Child, cover your mouth when you cough!"

Nina: "I'm not a child. I'm Nina Sophia."

I'm done. Somebody come and get her please.

At the store checkout with Nina today she offered to grab one of the bags from the cashier. The cashier said, "Thank you, Baby!"

You already know . . .
#HerNameIsNinaSophia

Over the weekend, my family and I were invited to join close friends on a quest to walk to the top of Kennesaw Mountain. "It will be a nice leisurely walk," we were told. "Plus, it is beautiful outside!"

Convinced we could not pass up the invitation, we loaded up the kids and were off!

The last time our family had been to Kennesaw Mountain was more than two years ago when we visited as a way to celebrate Mother's Day. I was pregnant with Nina Sophia at the time, our fifth child, and secretly hoped the visit would encourage her to make her way into the world. Of course, Nina had plans of her own and did not come for another few weeks, closer to her due date. Nonetheless, the kids had a vague memory of visiting Kennesaw Mountain, but their memory did include a shuttle bus trip up and back down the mountain. Not so for this trip.

We all started out at the base of the mountain as a group but quickly broke into smaller groups as we proceeded towards the top. My husband had Josiah, our youngest, in the stroller and was taking the mountain by storm with his long strides.

Next, the children's Godfather was in the lead as he and our Godson, along with Joshua and Hannah gradually made their way towards the summit. The children's Godmother was next in our walking caravan while Nina Sophia and I brought up the rear.

I was bemused many times during our trek as I watched, coaxed, encouraged, and even pulled Nina to continue on our journey. Our experience reminded me of how we can feel with life: fully focused and on fire, while at other times frustrated and distracted.

Nina, like most of us, started out with a burst of energy. She ran, even hopped at times, full of excitement, as she watched other walkers and their families pass us on both sides. Her high energy and positive disposition was quickly tested.

As we continued, her gait slowed, and I could see irritation and frustration begin to take the place of the excitement and energy that had been present only moments ago. Other members of our party began to become faint images as the distance between us grew.

"C'mon, Nina! Let's go! We can do it!" I would say to her. She was not amused nor moved.

At times, Nina would simply stop in the middle of the path and refuse to go further until I was able to convince her to keep going. It was at these times when I had to think about her motivation. What would keep her going? Joshua and Hannah were always far-off figures in front of us and I told her that if she kept going, we would eventually catch up to them.

That worked for a few moments until she stopped again. I fought the urge to give into the frustration she was displaying and tried to think of other ways to keep her motivated.

At one point, there was a couple who came from behind us with their dog, Ginger. Ginger was a cute little dog and the couple, seeing me struggle to convince Nina to continue, asked Nina if she wanted to pet Ginger. As Ginger kept moving, Nina moved along with her in an attempt to touch her. "Thank you," I mouthed to them, as the five of us took several more steps towards our goal. They nodded and smiled in silent understanding. They eventually passed us, but in that brief moment, they had assisted us with our overall goal.

I believe God sends reminders in the form of people to encourage us on our journeys and to let us know that we are not alone.

That brief interaction was also a reminder to monitor my motivation. While on the mountain, our goal was to reach the summit which caused me to think of multiple ways to motivate Nina. I have life goals as well and I have to find ways to motivate myself to keep my "eyes on the prize."

Whether it is an upcoming date night with my hubby or with one of our kids, or a chance to enjoy a new experience, it is absolutely *OK* to change my motivators as long as they assist with getting me closer to my goals. The same way I had to change Nina's motivators.

Throughout our journey, Nina asked repeatedly for her father, whom she could not see. I kept telling her that he was just up ahead and that if we kept going, he would be there waiting for her with open arms.

She would begin to trudge further a few more steps, with a renewed sense of hope and motivation. I wondered how many times our lives are just like this, where we ask for our Heavenly Father because we are in need or distressed and cannot see Him? Nina's call for her father reminded me that our Heavenly Father is ever present, not too far from us, and always waiting. And at times, clearing the path before us, ensuring our journey is safe.

There were several instances where I considered slinging Nina. No, not off the path but onto my back, of course! I imagined it would be easier just to have her on my back. Easier for her, because she would have the comfort of riding instead of walking and easier for me, because I would not have to continue to pull her along. There was, however, a larger part of me that wanted to see if she could actually make it all the way to the top.

As a parent, the temptation to keep my children from experiencing discomfort is great. I want to protect them and keep them from experiencing any emotion that hinders their smiles.

In that moment, I was reminded of the story of the butterfly where the danger of opening the cocoon too soon prevents the butterfly from developing strong wings. This reminder and my previous lower back issues kept me from putting Nina on my back. Onward, we walked!

In an effort to keep Nina's mind focused, I pointed out the beautiful scenery along the path. From the far-reaching views of Atlanta to the fresh waters cascading over the chiseled stone.

Thankfully, these slight distractions served as a form of reprieve and did not take us off our path. Sometimes in life, we become distracted by things, people, activities, etc., and end up in places that were not a part of our original journey. Some distractions can be helpful if they are used to redirect and keep you on your journey.

We had not thought about the provisions which were needed for our walk since visiting Kennesaw Mountain was a spur of the moment decision. Needless to say, as walkers and joggers passed us with their water bottles, Nina looked at them with longing in her eyes and asked me for water. My heart sank because I didn't have any water to give her. I told her that we were going to get some soon if she continued to walk with Mommy. While Nina dragged her now heavy-laden feet, another walker overheard our conversation and offered a bottle of water to us.

I thanked her profusely and noticed how excited and lively Nina became. While I could have beaten myself up for not thinking about our need for water, I instead chose to focus on how, once again, God sent a reminder in the form of a stranger. I was also thankful that the stranger chose to offer assistance instead of harsh judgement and from afar. God hears our requests, even the seemingly small ones.

When we finally rounded that last bend and could hear Joshua and Hannah calling out to us from the lookout point, there was such a sense of satisfaction and accomplishment that rose in me at that moment. I know I had the "OMG" look on my face when I finally caught my husband's gaze. Ultimately, we all had made it to the mountaintop.

I was most proud of Nina! Her little toddler legs had taken her all the way up Kennesaw Mountain!

To Nina's delight, she had a first-class seat on her daddy's shoulders for the ride down. I think I saw a smile on her face the entire trip down. She was finally with her daddy and we were heading home. Even though her journey was full of stops, starts, distractions, and long pauses, she made it. In my book, that is what matters most...she made it.

From my trek with Nina, I was reminded that while on our journey, it is important to monitor our attitudes, motivation, and also to surround ourselves with those who will encourage us along the way. Another key lesson I learned from our walk is to ensure we are prepared for the journey at hand but if that preparation is not sufficient, learn from our mistakes and keep it moving. Most importantly, don't forget to enjoy the scenery. If we are so focused on what we do not have and what is causing that moment's frustration, we run the risk of missing the beauty of life around us. We can make it on our personal journeys.

Enjoy your journey and remember you are not alone.

CHAPTER NINE
Josiah David Reese – Our Miracle Baby

While at our community fall costume party, I took Hannah to the rest room with Josiah on my hip.

Little girl: "Is he special ed?"

Hannah: "Yes, because they had to take his heart out and fix it. He has a scar now on his chest. That's why he is special ed."

Little girl: "Oh wow! I really like special ed kids. I wish I was special ed."

Hannah: "Yeah. And my mom had breast cancer."

All our business just out in the streets! Lol!

#Kids. #TheirPerspectives

Despite his rocky beginning, it has been wonderful getting to know our son, Josiah.

At 19 weeks of gestation, we went in for our detailed anatomy appointment full of cheer and excitement, as we anticipated learning the gender of our sixth child. We'd been through this type of visit numerous times before, but due to the amount of time the Tech spent on the area of the heart; I knew something was not quite right.

While I was at work the call came in. "Mrs. Reese, we discovered some abnormalities with your baby's heart. We need you to come in for more testing." Immediately, I was struck with fear and a sinking feeling in my stomach. I hung up the phone and went to a co-worker's office to seek prayer. Tears flowed as we grasped hands asking God to intervene with His peace.

Our trip to the doctor's office was a somber one. "There is a hole in your son's heart which needs to be repaired. We will need to conduct an amniocentesis to be certain of the cause."

I reached for my husband's hand as tears slowly rolled down my cheeks. I chose to remain calm even though I had never had an amniocentesis during any of my other pregnancies. The testing revealed there were a few issues with our son's heart ...and something else.

"Mr. and Mrs. Reese, there is a 99% chance that your son has Down Syndrome and we won't truly know the concerns and limitations of his heart until he is born."

The words fell from the doctor's lips onto the floor, splattering like a rotten tomato. It was difficult to focus on the rest of the words that were floating into the air. I kept rubbing my stomach and praying over our unborn child. "God . . . please . . ."

Over the next few weeks, we prayed, we researched, we talked, we cried, and we prayed some more. We knew it was important to enlist the support of family and friends, so we slowly began the process of sharing what we were told with those who were close to us. I remember not wanting to accept what the doctor said and clung to the hope that there was a 1% chance that our baby boy was going to be just fine.

Friday, May 8, 2015, I went in for a routine maternity check-up and was told to get to the hospital because there was fluid around our son's heart. The doctor wanted to begin the delivery process before we were forced to make some hasty decisions. Josiah's due date was not until much later that month. I checked in late that evening and began the wait for Josiah.

Unfortunately, my body was not quite ready to release Josiah and the wait turned out to be much longer than we had anticipated. We thought he was going to be born on the 10th, which happened to be Mother's Day, but that was not the case. A number of different techniques were tried to get my body to respond to the induction process, but nothing seemed to work. Josiah's heart rate dipped twice, and we were informed that if it dipped again, he would have to be delivered via C-section.

His heart rate dipped again, and the room suddenly became a flurry of activity. The hospital staff whisked around me and my husband Steve, to prepare us for delivery and surgery. Our five children and my mom were in the delivery room with us, our tradition, and I could see the look of alarm on their faces as I was being wheeled out of the room and they were being ushered to a sitting area. This was not the way it was supposed to be!

I could see my husband's slightly tear-streaked face as I was rushed passed him to the operating room.

"You're going to be ok," one of the staff members whispered to me while patting my arm. "We do these procedures on a daily basis." All five of my other children were delivered vaginally. Needless to say, I was full of mixed emotions which included being exhausted and just wanting him here, safely.

It all happened so quickly, he was lifted out of my body and offered for us to see. On May 11, 2015 Josiah David Reese made his grand entrance into this world. Finally!!

We were told that heart surgery was not immediately needed but he had to remain in the Neonatal Intensive Care Unit (NICU) after his birth, due to the complications during delivery.

Leaving the hospital without him was one of the most difficult things I have ever had to do, even though I knew he was receiving the best care. We visited the hospital daily and asked regularly when he would be released to go home. Before he could be discharged, we were told he had to be able to breathe on his own, pass the car seat test, and gain weight.

There were initial concerns about Josiah's hearing, but he eventually passed all testing. He was in NICU for a total of three weeks.

Subsequent visits to the doctor after discharge indicated surgery was imminent but they wanted to give him time to grow. At four months, Josiah underwent open heart surgery. Once again, he was in NICU and had to remain in the hospital. When I saw him for the first time after surgery, my heart tore a little because he looked so small, helpless, and sweet. My little man.

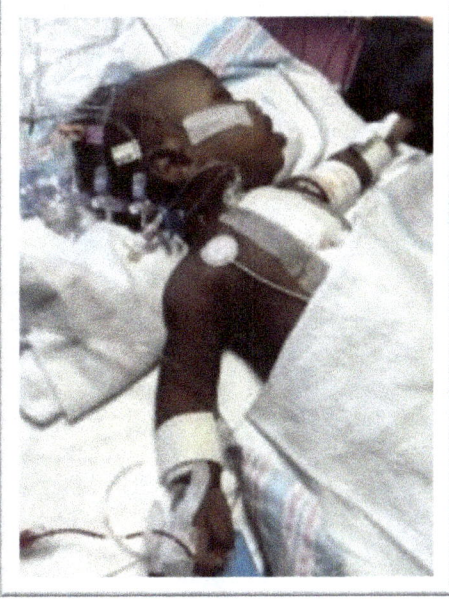

We soon realized that Josiah was a fighter, a "Little Warrior," as his maternal grandma affectionately calls him. His smile was and continues to be contagious and his laugh is so cute! We cannot imagine our lives without him.

What about the Down Syndrome (DS) diagnosis? DS is NOT our son. Josiah has some characteristics associated with DS including delayed growth in certain areas, but we do not box him in by a diagnosis. Yes, we remain informed about his growth and development, but we choose to focus on his abilities and not limit him before he even has a chance.

When we first received the news, I will admit, I was greatly disheartened. I did not want to hear it, discuss it, or accept it. In fact, if I am truly honest, Josiah was almost a statistic, a child never born since the doctor offered the option to end the pregnancy. I thank God for His grace, peace, and mercy. I would not have been able to live with a decision to abort, even though it was an option freely offered.

Each time I look at Josiah, I am humbled by God's selection of us to be his parents. He is an active baby, crawling around to keep up with his siblings and grabbing everything! He is also extremely vocal and enjoys chatting, especially with his daddy. He is so busy!! He is a gift...a gift for our family and for the world. I love me some Josiah David Reese! Sometimes your greatest gift and blessing comes in a package you had not imagined. Do not allow fear to cause you to miss out on something beautiful.

CHAPTER TEN
Prayers for Our Children

These are prayers I created to cover our children in prayer.

I used Stormie Omartian's "The Power of a Praying Parent" Study Guide as a resource.

#ProtectOurSeed

#IBelieveTheChildrenAreOurFuture

#PrayingParents

Day 1: Becoming a Praying Parent

"For our struggle is not against flesh and blood, but against the rules, against the authorities, against the powers of this dark world and against the spiritual forces of evil in the heavenly realms." Ephesians 6:12

Father, as we commit this month to praying for our children we begin by praying for ourselves as parents. We release any feelings of guilt and condemnation we have felt in the area of parenting. We thank You for covering any mistakes we may have made and for Your grace and mercy. You have selected each of us to serve as a parent. We do not take that for granted and know that we can do all things through You, even being the best Mom and Dad our children need.

Ephesians 6:12 tells us that we do not wrestle against flesh and blood and with that knowledge we stand with our armor of God ready for the fight. We know that in James 4:7 we are to resist the enemy and he will flee. So, we are joined together as parents prepared to successfully resist the enemy's plans for our children. Give us discernment on what to pray specifically as it pertains to our children. In Jesus' name. Amen!

#LetsDoThis. #CoveringOurSeed

Day 2: Releasing Our Children into God's Hands

"Children are a heritage from the Lord, offspring a reward from him." Psalm 127:3

Heavenly Father, thank You for our gifts, our children. You tell us in your word that children are a heritage from You and that they are a fruit of the womb (Psalms 127:3). Today, we release our children to You. Just as in the photo of the Lion King, the enemy will be lurking nearby. We know our children will be in good hands and that You love each of them more than we do.

We rebuke the spirit of worry and know that You did not give us a spirit of fear but of power and of love and of a sound mind (II Timothy 1:7). We ask You to be in control of our children's lives and release any reason that would cause difficulty in fully releasing them to you.

You tell us in Isaiah 65:23 that we shall not labor in vain and that we did not bring forth our children for trouble. They shall be descendants blessed of the Lord!

In Jesus' name! Amen!

Day 3: Securing Protection from Harm

"Whoever dwells in the shelter of the Most High will rest in the shadow of the Almighty." Psalm 91:1

Lord, we pray for protection from all harm, danger, and disasters for our children. Reveal to us any hidden dangers. May we exercise discernment when our children express a fear to us. Grant us a supernatural ability to truly hear any concerns and to respond appropriately.

You tell us in Psalm 112:7 that we will not be afraid of evil tidings and that our hearts will be steadfast, trusting in You. Show us anything we need to do to increase our children's safety.

We thank You in advance for peace in this area. You have been a shelter for (your child's name), [Amali, Azaan, Joshua, Hannah, Nina and Josiah] and we will trust in the shelter of Your wings as described in Psalm 61:3-4. We will never be shaken!

In Jesus' name. Amen!

Day 4: Feeling Loved and Accepted

"We love because he first loved us." I John 4:19

Have you told your child(ren) how much you love them?

Do they believe you?

Lord, You tell us in Isaiah 41:9 that You have chosen us and not cast us away. Show us how to help our children believe that they are chosen by You and that You will always be with them. Reveal to us how our own childhood experiences may be influencing how we show love to our children and what to do if those influences are not positive. We absolutely want our children to feel loved so give us the courage to ask them how they want to be loved and the willingness to follow through in creative ways.

Enable us to address any rejection issues our children may feel and to exercise discernment to determine if the concern is real. We cover our children in advance for any uncomfortable social situations they may encounter where they may not feel accepted. Help us to remind them of their identity, Father, and that they are fearfully and wonderfully made (Psalm 139:14).

In Jesus' name. Amen!

Day 5: Establishing an Eternal Future

"For our light and momentary troubles are achieving for us an eternal glory that far outweighs them all." 2 Corinthians 4:17

In John 6:40 we are reminded that, "everyone who believes in Him may have everlasting life." Lord, we want this for our children. We pray for any of our children who have not yet accepted You as their Savior and ask for the courage to talk freely about You and Your goodness with them.

Help us to see how our own relationship with You affects our children's relationships with You. We desire our relationship to be an inspiration to our children to draw them closer to You. We understand the spiritual value of an eternal future and we want our children to have access to that value. We want them to have the power that is described in John 14:12-14 where whatever is asked in Your name You will do for those who believe in You.

Lord, thank You for speaking to the hearts of our children.

In Jesus' name. Amen!

Day 6: Honoring Parents and Resisting Rebellion

"Honor your father and your mother, so that you may live long in the land of the Lord your God is giving you." Exodus 20:12

Lord, we rebuke the spirit of rebellion in our children. Ephesians 6:1-3 instructs us to, "honor our mother and father so that it will go well and we may enjoy long life." We want our children to enjoy long lives and pray against any idols that may be in their hearts. Instead of rebellion we pray for obedience and submission. Instead of pride we pray for humility. Replace selfishness with selflessness.

Father, we know that delayed obedience is a form of disobedience and we pray for guidance on ways to stop that behavior in our children. We realize that we struggle not against flesh and blood and therefore are prepared to put on our whole armor daily for our children (Ephesians 6:10-18).

We thank You in advance for rescuing our children from the hands of their enemies (Nehemiah 9:26-27).

In Jesus' name. Amen!

Day 7: Maintaining Good Family Relationships

"Let us therefore make every effort to do what leads to peace and to mutual edification." Romans 14:19

Father today we are seeking prayer for the ability of our children to maintain good family relationships. If there are strained, fractured, or severed situations in our families today, we ask You to restore them. We know that breakdowns in familial relationships can negatively affect our children and we pray for protection against that negativity.

Lord, You tell us in Romans 14:19 to pursue the things which make for peace. Help us to be examples of peacemakers in our families, illustrating the power of prayer over damaged relationships. We cover the key relationships in our children's lives which are especially crucial to our children's happiness. We desire lasting and loving relationships with each one of these people. Help us to reflect compassion for our family members, to be tenderhearted and courteous as you instruct us in I Peter 3:8, not returning evil for evil.

We thank You in advance for the peace and happiness our children will experience in this area.

In Jesus' name. Amen!

Day 8: Attracting Godly Friends and Role Models

"He who walks with wise men will be wise, but the companion of fools will be destroyed." Proverbs 13:20

Heavenly Father we come before you in the spirit realm to cover our children's ability to attract Godly friends and role models. You tell us in Your word that "the righteous should choose his friends carefully for the way of the wicked leads them astray." We pray for limited to no contact with those individuals who bring out the worst in our children. We know that blessed is the one who walks not in the counsel of the ungodly, but instead delights in the law of the Lord.

We thank You for those wise friends and models for our children; strengthen the ones already established and bring new ones that need to be replaced. We pray (enter your child's name) [Amali, Azaan, Joshua, Josiah, Hannah and Nina] will love their enemies and always seek to forgive easily as described in Matthew 5:44. Lastly, we pray for any relationship that is troubling or upsetting our children. Make it clear to us if we need to intervene or not on behalf of our children.

In Jesus' name. Amen!

Day 9: Developing a Hunger for the Things of God

"Oh taste and see that the Lord is good; Blessed is the man who trusts in Him!" Psalm 34:8

Lord, we pray our own lives reflect a healthy fear of You in our children's eyes. We pray against any influences that threaten to draw their attention away from the things of You. Father, take away the desire for those things that compete with You for our children's attention. You tell us in Proverbs 10:27 that the "fear of the Lord prolongs days, but the years of the wicked will be shortened." Give our children a healthy fear of You, Lord. May they hate what You hate and desire what You desire for their lives.

Help us to teach, instruct, train, and encourage our children in the things of God. We know that there is no want to those who fear You, Father, and that those who seek You shall not lack any good thing (Psalm 34:9-10).

We don't want our children to lack any good thing! We pray that (your child's name) [Amali, Azaan, Joshua, Hannah, Nina and Josiah] will taste and see that You are good and have a greater hunger for You!

In Jesus' name. Amen!

Day 10: Being the Person God Created

"For You formed my inward parts; You covered me in my mother's womb." Psalm 139:13

Heavenly Father, thank You for the gifts you have bestowed upon us in the form of our children. May we help them to understand who You have created them to be. Help us to nurture their God-given gifts and talents and for them to use them to further Your kingdom. Father, whenever we see our children striving to be something they were not created to be or straining to do something that will never fulfill them, remind us to be gentle in our approach. We want our children to know with certainty that they belong to You as described in Isaiah 44:5.

We rebuke the spirit of comparison in our children's lives and in ours as well because we recognize the impact unfavorable comparison to others has on our children's attitudes about themselves. Lord, we want our children to experience the blessings You promise in Isaiah 44:3-4 for those who thirst for You, blessings that span generations.

Thank You in advance for these things we ask, in your son's Jesus' name. Amen!

Day 11: Following Truth, Rejecting Lies

"The Lord detests lying lips, but he delights in people who are trustworthy." Proverbs 12:22

Lord we know that "lying lips are an abomination" to You and "those who deal truthfully" are Your delight (Proverbs 12:22). Help us to teach our children not to lie. Lord, if any of us as parents struggle with this issue, we pray for Your grace and mercy as You deal with us and convict our hearts to do better. Help us to communicate to our children the severity of telling lies and the rewards of telling the truth. Reveal the root issue of wanting to protect themselves by lying and the benefits of being set free. Pour out Your Spirit of truth on our children as described in John 14:16-17.

We decree that our children's hearts belong to You and no parts will be surrendered to the enemy, the father of lies. Reveal to us any time our children tell a lie so that nothing will be hidden. Help us as parents to establish appropriate discipline when lying does occur. We thank You for our children's ability to follow truth and reject lies.

In Jesus' name! Amen!

Day 12: Enjoying a Life of Health and Healing

"And the prayer offered in faith will make the sick person well; the Lord will raise them up. If they have sinned, they will be forgiven." James 5:16

Lord, our hearts ache when our children are sick. You tell us in Matthew 8:17 that your son "took our infirmities and bore our sicknesses." We pray for healing today, Father, for all physical ailments that are affecting our children. We thank You in advance for answering our prayers in this area. Lord, sometimes we do not see immediate healing. In those instances, we know we "walk by faith, not by sight" (II Corinthians 5:7). We know of countless accounts in the Bible where people's faith was key to their healing.

Remind us to have faith in all matters especially in the area of healing and health. Lord, if our faith lacks, increase it. Give our children a faith strong enough to believe for Your healing power to flow through their lives on an ongoing basis. We pray for supernatural healing, specifically in the area of (insert your concern) [migraines, down syndrome, allergies and athletic injuries]. We also pray a hedge of protection against any future sicknesses developing or injuries happening. James 5:15-16 tells us that the "prayer of faith will save the sick" and the "fervent prayer of a righteous man (or parent) avails much." We are fervently praying!

In Jesus' name. Amen!

Day 13: Having the Motivation for Proper Body Care

"Do you not know that your bodies are temples of the Holy Spirit, who is in you, whom you have received from God? You are not your own;" I Corinthians 6:19

Lord, we know exactly what it's like to struggle with poor eating or exercise habits, smoking, drinking, or other kinds of neglect or abuse to our bodies. For these reasons, we are taking a stance as praying parents to pray our children will have the discipline, self-control, and wisdom to eat right, exercise regularly and take good care of their bodies. We know that our bodies are temples and that we are to honor God with our bodies. Help us to convey that concept to our children. May they take hold at an early age the importance of honoring their bodies.

Father, as we cover our children in this area, help us to remember our own bodies so that we can serve as positive examples for our children. Help us to discern quickly any tendencies our children exhibit in the form of abuse or neglect with their physical bodies. You tell us in I Corinthians 10:31 that "whatever we eat or drink to do so all for the glory of God." We know that if "anyone destroys God's temple, God will destroy that person; for God's temple is sacred" (I Corinthians 3:17). In light of this, we wholeheartedly pray for our children to take care of their bodies.

In Jesus' name. Amen!

Day 14: Instilling the Desire to Learn

"The fear of the Lord is the beginning of knowledge, but fools despise wisdom and instruction." Proverbs 1:7

Heavenly Father, we want our children to succeed. We know that success depends on the ability and desire to learn. Today, we are praying for that ability and desire to be fostered in our children. We do not want them to despise wisdom and instruction. Father, if we have observed any issues in this area, we seek discernment on how to address this issue as quickly as possible. We know that happiness is associated with wisdom and understanding (Proverbs 2:13) and we want our children to experience the joy and rewards that comes from having wisdom.

Father, we understand that You are the ultimate teacher of our children and that You promise to give them peace (Isaiah 54:13). We stand in agreement for this peace for our children and thank You in advance for the gains our children will experience as a result of wisdom and understanding. We are not parents of fools!

In Jesus' name! Amen!

Day 15: Identifying God-Given Gifts and Talents

"For the gifts and the calling of God are irrevocable."
Romans 11:29

Lord, thank you for the natural gifts, abilities and talents You have placed in our children. Help us to be keenly aware of how to encourage their further development. If there are other gifts and talents in our children that we have not seen, please reveal them to us and with clarity. As parents, we want to nurture, protect and develop those talents. You tell us in Romans 18:16 that "a man's gift makes room for him and brings him before great men."

Lord, we pray that the gifts and talents You have placed in (your child's name) [Amali, Azaan, Joshua, Hannah, Nina and Josiah] will make room for them and bring them before great people. Thank You, God, that our children come short in no gift and that they are enriched in everything (I Corinthians 1:4-7). Give us a glimpse of our children's potential for greatness. Help our children to excel in their God-given gifts and to be recognized and appreciated by others as described in Proverbs 22:29.

Lord, thank You for blessing our children in this area.

In Jesus' name. Amen!

#OurChildrenRock #PrayingParents

Day 16: Learning to Speak Life

"Death and life are in the power of the tongue, and those who love it will eat its fruit." Proverbs 18:21

Dear Heavenly Father, good morning! Today we pray for our children's ability to speak life. We know that, "he who guards his mouth preserves his life, but he who opens wide his lips shall have destruction" (Proverbs 13:3). We do not want destruction to come upon our children! We pray our children recognize at an early age that words have power and they can either speak life or death into a situation. May they choose to speak life. If for some reason the words they speak are not positive, may they quickly recognize their error and change their speech. Lord, if our children speak negatively about themselves reveal to us the reasons why those words were said so we can address the matter effectively and as quickly as possible.

Help us to encourage our children to be open and honest about their negative emotions and thoughts and show them how to pray about them. If our children are not open and honest help us to encourage more open sharing. Your word tells us that "a good man out of the good treasure of his heart brings forth good things and an evil man out of the evil treasure brings forth evil things" (Matthew 12:35). We pray for our children's hearts to enable the flow of good things. Let the words of (your child's name) [Amali's, Azaan's, Joshua's, Hannah's, Nina's, and Josiah's] mouths and the meditation of their hearts be acceptable in your sight. In Jesus' holy name. Amen!

#PrayingParents

Day 17: Staying Attracted to Holiness and Purity

"For God did not call us to uncleanness, but to holiness." 1 Thessalonians 4:7

Heavenly Father, thank you for allowing us to submit our petitions to You regarding our children. Today, we are praying for our children's attitudes towards living a holy and pure life. Lord, we know that instruction begins at home so reveal to us any areas where we need to adjust our own attitudes towards living a holy and pure life. Father, we pray for positive role models who also encourage our children to be attracted to holiness and purity. We know that You, Lord, are the ultimate teacher and that holiness begins with a love for You. May our children thirst for Your love and earnestly seek You out at an early age. Help us to encourage our children to keep themselves pure. We pray for a new beginning for those who may have gotten off track for whatever reason and thank you for the grace and mercy you have shown in their lives.

Proverbs 20:11 tells us that, "even a child is known by his deeds, whether what he does is pure and right." We pray our children's deeds are pleasing in your sight, Lord. We know that the pure in heart are blessed (Matthew 5:8) and we desire this blessing for our children. We pray that (your child's name) [Amali, Azaan, Joshua, Hannah, Nina and Josiah] will ascend into the hill of the Lord and receive blessing (Psalm 24:3-5). Let no one despise (your child's name) [Amali's, Azaan's, Joshua's, Hannah's, Nina's and Josiah's] youth but that they are examples in "word, in conduct, in love, in spirit, in faith and in purity" (I Timothy 4:12). In Jesus' name. Amen!

Day 18: Praying Through a Child's Room

"And you shall take the anointing oil and anoint the tabernacle and all that is in it; and you shall hallow it and all its utensils, and it shall be holy." Exodus 40:9

Our children's rooms should be a sanctuary, a safe haven. Father, we cover our children's rooms today. If our children have nightmares, unexplained fears, or periods of aggressive behavior, please give us discernment on what the issue may be and how we can immediately address it. Lord, reveal to us if there is anything unholy in our children's rooms. Whether it's a stuffed animal, electronic device, or a book, bring it to our attention. May we cover every item, every window and doorway in our children's rooms with anointing oil.

We stand together right now, Father, in the spirit realm covering our children's rooms in prayer. We want our children's rooms to be a place of refuge and safety, therefore we guard against anything that is in their room that is not of You, Lord. Father we pray that (your child's name) [Amali, Azaan, Joshua, Hannah, Nina and Josiah] will behave wisely and in a perfect way.

I pray they will walk within our home with a perfect heart and not set anything wicked before their eyes (Psalm 101:2-4). Remind us to maintain purity and holiness throughout our homes for the protection of our children.

In Jesus' name. Amen.

Day 19: Enjoying Freedom from Fear

"For the Spirit God gave us does not make us timid, but gives us power, love and self-discipline." 2 Timothy 1:7

Do any of your fears manifest themselves in your children in any way?

Lord, we know that You did not give us a spirit of fear, but of power and of love and of a sound mind (II Timothy 1:7). Help us to be aware of any fears that our children may have. In Luke 10:19 You gave us authority to trample "over all the power of the enemy" and so today in the spirit realm we STOMP on anything that may cause fear in our children. We stomp out insecurities, low self-esteem, the opinions of others and generational curses! There is no fear in love; but perfect love casts out fear (I John 4:18) and we thank you, Father, for Your perfect love. The Lord is (your child's name) [Amali's, Azaan's, Joshua's, Hannah's, Nina's and Josiah's] light and salvation (Psalm 27:1) and they shall not fear anyone or anything. We pray that You will cover our children as described in Psalm 91:4-6 whenever they are afraid. We thank You for the victory our children will experience in this area. In Jesus' name. Amen!

Want extra protection in this area? Write out Psalm 91 and insert your child's name in every space.

"Surely He shall deliver Amali from the snare of the fowler…He shall cover Amali with His feathers…"

Day 20: Receiving a Sound Mind

"Be alert and of sober mind. Your enemy the devil prowls around like a roaring lion looking for someone to devour." 1 Peter 5:8

Lord, today we pray against our children ever struggling with confusion, the inability to stay focused, difficulty understanding things appropriate for their age or negative thinking. We present any concerns or fears we have about the development of our children's minds to you. We know that Isaiah 26:3 tells us that You will keep our children in "perfect peace whose mind is stayed on You." Remind us to encourage our children to praise You regularly to combat self-centeredness. Remind us to encourage our children to be thankful and to glorify You as God on a regular basis (Romans 1:21).

Father, we seek life and peace for our children and therefore want them to be spiritually minded as described in Romans 8:6. For You have given (your child's name) [Amali, Azaan, Joshua, Hannah, Nina and Josiah] a sound mind (II Timothy 1:7).

In Jesus' name. Amen!

Day 21: Inviting the Joy of the Lord

"I will give thanks to the Lord because of his righteousness; I will sing the praises of the name of the Lord Most High." Psalm 7:17

When you observe your child's face, does it most often reflect peace and joy, or is it frequently depressed, angry, sad, moody, or troubled?

Good morning, Father! Today we are praying our children have the joy of the Lord. We pray that You will show (your child's name) [Amali, Azaan, Joshua, Hannah, Nina and Josiah] the path of life so they will experience the fullness of joy (Psalm 16:11). We pray that You, the God of hope, will fill (your child's name) [Amali, Azaan, Joshua, Hannah, Nina and Josiah] with all joy and peace (Romans 15:13). Lord, we know this is the day that You have made for (your child's name) [Amali, Azaan, Joshua, Hannah, Nina and Josiah]. We pray that they will rejoice in it! (Psalm 118:24). We pray that our children manifest the fruit of the spirit as described in Galatians 5:22-23-love, joy, peace, longsuffering, kindness, goodness, faithfulness, gentleness, and self-control. We pray that our children learn how to be content in every stage of their lives (Philippians 4:11) and that they will have merry hearts ♡ (Proverbs 15:15).

Father, we pray that You will bless (your child's name) [Amali, Azaan, Joshua, Hannah, Nina and Josiah] and keep them and shine upon them (Numbers 6:24-26). We pray for healthy and positive attitudes. In Jesus' name. Amen!

Day 22: Destroying an Inheritance of Family Bondage

"It is for freedom that Christ has set us free. Stand firm, then, and do not let yourselves be burdened again by a yoke of slavery." Galatians 5:1

*Excerpts of this prayer were taken from a prayer shared by Bishop Dale C. Bronner on social media.

Is there a trait, characteristic, or habit you or your child's other parent have which you would not like to see your child emulate or inherit?

Heavenly Father, we come to You today to cover our children's inheritance. We pray against any negative tendency that runs in our families such as laziness, irresponsibility, self-pity, anger, unforgiveness, bitterness, gossiping, coldness, or being critical. We pray against any sinful or destructive patterns of behavior on either side of our families which we do not want to touch our children's lives such as alcoholism, infidelity, lying, divorce, drugs, or poor money management.

God has given us the authority over all the power of the enemy and so we take that authority and break ALL the bondages over our families! We say that they have no part in our lives or in the lives of our children! We know we are children of God and our inheritance comes from Christ (Romans 8:15-17).

We proclaim right now to the enemy that our children are heirs of God. Once we confess our sins, God is faithful and just to "cleanse us from all unrighteousness" (I John 1:9. May our children be quick to confess their sins whenever needed. Christ has made us free from a "yoke of bondage" and we pray this freedom for our children (Galatians 5:1).

Father, we claim that (your child's name) [Amali, Azaan, Joshua, Hannah, Nina, and Josiah] are in Christ and they are a new creation; old things have passed away; behold, all things have become new (II Corinthians 5:17). We pray these things in Your mighty Son's majestic name. Amen!

Day 23: Avoiding Alcohol, Drugs, and Other Addictions

"For if you live according to the flesh, you will die; but if by the Spirit you put to death the misdeeds of the body, you will live." Romans 8:13

Lord, we pray our children will have the integrity of the upright to resist any temptation that the enemy puts in their path. We want our children to be built up in the truth of the Lord. We believe we have authority over all the power of the enemy and therefore we stand together breaking all strongholds in our children's lives through prayer. 🙏. No temptation has overtaken (your child's name) [Amali, Azaan, Joshua, Hannah, Nina and Josiah] except such is common to man; but God is faithful... and will also make the way of escape (I Corinthians 10:13).

Lord we pray that (your child's name) [Amali, Azaan, Joshua, Hannah, Nina and Josiah], will not live according to the flesh which brings death but will live by the Spirit (Romans 8:13). We pray our children love the Lord our God, obey His voice and cling to Him as described in Deuteronomy 30:20 to have long life. We pray for the Holy Spirit to help our children make right choices, choices for life, every day.

In Jesus' name. Amen!

Day 24: Rejecting Sexual Immorality

"So I say, walk by the Spirit, and you will not gratify the desires of the flesh." Galatians 5:16

Are you convinced of the need for sexual purity in your life and the lives of your children?

Father, we pray for sexual purity today for our children. We do not want the wholeness of their souls to be sacrificed because of giving place to the lust of the flesh (I Peter 2:11). We pray that our children walk wisely and not trust in their own hearts when dealing with sexual sin (Proverbs 28:26).

Even if our children have already stumbled into sexual immorality, we pray for them to live in sexual purity from now on and to count all trials as a testing of their faith (James 1:2-3).

Father, even as we pray for our children today, we ask for forgiveness for any traps of the enemy we have fallen into which have led to sexual immorality. We confess it to You Lord, even our thought life, so the enemy has no grounds for a stronghold in our lives.

May our children not be drawn away from You with their own desires and enticed (James 1:14-15) but instead may they seek after your righteousness. May they walk in the Spirit and be led by the Spirit for we know we cannot be with them at all times.

We pray that they avoid all works of the flesh such as adultery and fornication (Galatians 5:19-21) and instead operate in the fruit of the Spirit (Galatians 5:22) such as goodness and faithfulness. We ask these things in Jesus' name. Amen!

Want extra protection in this area? Write out a prayer asking God to help your child exhibit all the fruits of the Spirit while mentioning each one specifically.

Day 25: Finding the Perfect Mate

"Unless the Lord builds the house, they labor in vain who build it." Psalm 127:1

Lord, we know that You hate divorce. For this reason, we are covering our children and their ability to find perfect mates. We realize that marriages begin as simple relationships and therefore "the righteous should choose their friends carefully" (Proverbs 12:26). You tell us in Your word that we are not to be unequally yoked together with unbelievers (II Corinthians 6:14). We pray our children and their potential mates will have a shared love for Jesus Christ. If we have experienced divorce anywhere in our families, we pray to break that spirit over our children's lives. If divorce has not occurred, we pray to keep it far from our children. Father, we ask You to be in charge of our children's marriages.

We are praying that our children not only find the perfect mates but that they will not enter into marriage with expectations so high that their spouses can't live up to them. Give our children positive examples of what You envision for marriage. Father, reveal Your will to our children regarding their future mates. We do not cease to pray for (your child's name) [Amali, Azaan, Joshua, Hannah, Nina and Josiah], and ask that they may be filled with the knowledge of God's will in all wisdom and spiritual understanding (Colossians 1:9). In Jesus' name. Amen!

Day 26: Living Free of Unforgiveness

"But if you do not forgive others their sins, your Father will not forgive your sins." Matthew 6:15

Does forgiveness flow freely in your family or does unforgiveness have a place in one or more family members?

Heavenly Father, as we pray for our children's ability to live freely of unforgiveness, let us first start with ourselves. Help us to confess unforgiveness so we can be set free! Help us to know what true forgiveness looks like and to walk in that freedom. Keep us free from hidden unforgiveness in the future. We pray our children find it easy to forgive and let go of unforgiveness. If there is a specific area of unforgiveness in our children, reveal it to us and give us discernment on how to address it. You tell us in your word that if we forgive those who trespass against us, You will also forgive us (Matthew 6:14).

Let all bitterness, wrath, anger, clamor, and evil speaking be put away from (your child's name) [Amali, Azaan, Joshua, Hannah, Nina and Josiah] and may they instead be kind, tenderhearted and forgiving (Ephesians 4:31-32).

Father, we pray that our children offer love that suffers long and is kind; love that does not envy nor behave rudely but bears all things (I Corinthians 13:4-7). We pray that (your child's name) [Amali, Azaan, Joshua, Hannah, Nina and Josiah] who are Your holy and beloved children, will put on tender mercies, kindness, humility, meekness, and long suffering in order to forgive others (Colossians 3:12-13). In Jesus' name. Amen.

Day 27: Walking in Repentance

"He who covers his sins will not prosper, But whoever confesses and forsakes them will have mercy." Proverbs 28:13

Good morning, Lord! We are praying that our children are encouraged not to cover their sins. We pray You keep them from ever becoming comfortable with concealing their sins. Father, thank You for the times when their sin has been revealed by the look on their faces before it was discovered in their behavior. We know that even if they are able to hide sins from us, they cannot hide them from You (Psalm 69:5). Not only are we praying for the courage in our children to admit or confess their sin but we also want them to be repentant, to be sorry enough to not want to do it again. We want them to readily seek forgiveness from you, God. Search (your child's name) [Amali, Azaan, Joshua, Hannah, Nina and Josiah], O God, and know their hearts.

See if there is any wicked way in them and lead them in the way everlasting (Psalm 139:23-24). Create in (your child's name) [Amali, Azaan, Joshua, Hannah, Nina and Josiah] a clean heart ♡, O God, and renew a steadfast spirit within them (Psalm 51:10). We pray these things in Jesus' name. Amen.

Day 28: Breaking Down Ungodly Strongholds

"For there is nothing covered that will not be revealed, not hidden that will not be known." Luke 12:2

Father, reveal to us the truth of what is going on in our children's minds and lives. If we see any patterns of misbehaving such as dishonesty, deception, greed, selfishness, arrogance, or disobedience, help us to address those issues immediately and in love. God, we pray for You to destroy any strongholds the enemy wants to establish in our children's lives. Do not lead our children into temptation but deliver them from evil (Matthew 6:13).

We know we don't have to be suspicious of our children but instead we have to be wary of the enemy who is always lurking and waiting (I Peter 5:8). Father, we resist the enemy, on behalf of our children, and remain steadfast in the faith as described in I Peter 5:9. We will also remain sober and vigilant in protecting our children from the enemy's plans for he has no place in our children's lives!

In Jesus' name. Amen!

Day 29: Seeking Wisdom and Discernment

"If any of you lacks wisdom, let him ask of God, who gives to all liberally and without reproach, and it will be given to him." James 1:5

Good morning, Father! We pray for our children's abilities to make right choices and good decisions. We ask for wisdom for our children. We pray that wisdom will be in (your child's name) [Amali's, Azaan's, Joshua's, Hannah's, Nina's and Josiah's] hearts ♡ to deliver them from the way of evil (Proverbs 2:10-12). We know that the benefits of wisdom and understanding are countless including length of days, riches and honor and peace 👊 (Proverbs 3:13-18). We know that getting wisdom and understanding will bring promotion, honor, grace and a crown of glory (Proverbs 4:7-9).

In Proverbs 23:24-25 we learn that a wise child will bring delight to his/her parents. We are excited about that, Lord! We thank You for the ways in which we can obtain wisdom by receiving your words and treasuring your commands (Proverbs 2:1-7). We pray that our children will understand the value of wisdom and cry out for discernment, for we know You are a shield to those who walk uprightly; and You guard their paths (Proverbs 2:7-8). We thank you for being these for our children!

In Jesus' name. Amen!

Our FINAL Day!
Day 30: Growing in Faith

'Jesus turned and saw her. "Take heart, daughter," he said, "your faith has healed you." And the woman was healed at that moment.' Matthew 9:22

Heavenly Father, thank You for hearing our prayers regarding our children over the past 29 days. Our prayer today is for their ability to grow in faith. May our children see our own faith as strong examples. We know that all things are possible for those who believe (Matthew 9:22). We know that those who doubt are like the waves of the sea, driven and tossed by the wind (James 1:6).

We pray our children do not doubt and instead abide in faith, hope and love as according to I Corinthians 13:13. Father, if there are times when our children's faith wavers, remind them of Your steadfast love and Your ability to care for all of their needs. Help us to encourage their faith by pointing out Your presence in ALL things. We pray our children exhibit strong faith when faced with difficult circumstances. Your word tells us that as long as our children have faith the size of a mustard seed, then they will be able to speak to the hardships that seem like mountains in their lives and that nothing will be impossible for them (Matthew 17:20).

Lord, we thank You for our children's faith! In Jesus' name. Amen.

Day 31: 🎵 C E L E B R A T I O N Time.

Come On! It's time to celebrate! There's a party going on over here...it's time to celebrate! 🎉 🎵.

"Bring the fattened calf...
Let's have a feast and celebrate." Luke 15:23

Today we are celebrating our children! Share your praise reports, your favorite pics of your children or how proud you are of them on IG, FB, Twitter and snapchat. Flood social media with the power of positivity for your children!

We've learned at our church that what you focus on gets bigger. So, while all our prayers for our children may not have been answered yet, we are focusing on the positive today.

CHAPTER ELEVEN
They Said I Have Cancer; but, I Say, "Cancer Does Not Have Me!"

Nina: "Where are your breasts Mommy?"

Me: "The doctor took them."

Nina: "And flushed them down the toilet?"

Ummmmmm . . .

#NinaSophia #CloseButNotQuite

At times, being a mother gives me the motivation to keep living. This is especially true during exceptionally difficult times. While I was lying in my bed, my fingers came across an unfamiliar mass.

"Honey, does this feel weird to you?" My husband's fingers carefully searched the area.

"You probably need to contact the doctor first thing on Monday morning," he said in a concerned tone.

After the initial breast exam, I was scheduled for a detailed mammogram and an ultrasound.

"...And . . . stop breathing . . ." This phrase was repeated several times as the technician took pictures of my carefully placed breast. She returned to my side to reposition it. She was so close to me that a strand of her hair became caught in my lipstick, helpless, much like I felt at that moment.

A piece of my anatomy, my left breast, which had served in a variety of capacities throughout my life, was under inspection. It had nourished six children, enticed during intimate moments, and offered support to beautifully flowing dresses. Now it was being squashed, stretched, pulled, prodded, and pushed.

"And stop breathing," the tech said again. As I held my breath, I wondered what fate awaited me.

"Mrs. Reese, your results are abnormal. We need you to return for a biopsy."

While the Breast Care Advocate explained the procedure, my mind wandered. "What if it is the worse-case scenario? What if I have a limited amount of time left to . . .? What would I want to do with my remaining time to live?

Will the kids remember me? Will my husband still find me attractive if I begin to look sickly? What will people say about my life?"

"Mrs. Reese, do you have any questions? Mrs. Reese?" The Breast Care Advocate's voice penetrated my thoughts and brought me back to this new, sobering reality.

"Um . . . no . . . I understand," I said tuning back in.

During the days leading up to the biopsy, I experienced sporadic periods of crying. I spent a great deal of energy, however, keeping my mind on Christ and channeling positive thoughts and vibes. Overall, the procedure was not painful. It certainly did not compare to child labor and birth experiences, that's for sure!

The popping noise the biopsy tool made was unbelievably annoying. "I'm going to remove some tissue in 3...2...1," the doctor said. POP! The sound was similar to the noise elongated lighters make. All the while, I had the song, "Good, Good Father," playing in my mind as a few tears made their way down the side of my face.

"Mrs. Reese, your tissue will be sent off for analysis and we should have your results by next Tuesday." It was Thursday. On Saturday, I received the call.

"Mrs. Reese, your results have returned. I tried to reach you on Friday but did not want to leave a message. They are not what we had hoped."

My heart immediately sank and my palms became sweaty as I reached for my husband's leg who was seated next to me on the couch. "I have you on speaker phone so my husband can hear the news as well."

"The mass is cancerous. Thankfully, it is in stage one and is measuring at a small amount. The type of cancer you have is called invasive mammary carcinoma. It is appearing both in your ducts and in your lobes." I looked at my husband as he sat up to hear the doctor more clearly.

"We have you scheduled to come in on Tuesday to speak with the doctor during a consult. I want to stress that the focus should be on the size and the fact that it is a low grade."

Once the call ended, my hubby turned to me and asked, "First, how do you feel and then what do you think?" I said, "There are a number of emotions right now. Relief. Concern. Amazement. Disbelief. My life has changed forever."

On Tuesday, our senses were on high alert as we waited for our visit with the surgeon. We knew we were in good hands when we arrived, when the attending nurse introduced herself to us as, "Grace." We hear you, Lord!

The consultation went better than expected and the surgeon offered some comfort in an otherwise very unsettling situation. We asked a number of questions and gained a greater understanding of my case. We were again told to focus on the fact that it was caught early and the mass is very small.

Surgery and treatment will be scheduled soon. My cancer survivor journey has begun.

Cancer does not have me!

Healing Like a Fighter

"The results from your tissue analysis have returned. Your right breast and lymph nodes were clear. The other masses near the cancerous tissue were benign. Mrs. Reese, your pathology report is all clear!"

It took a moment for the words to sink in. My pathology report was clear! Really? No radiation or chemotherapy is needed? Praise God!

It all still seemed so surreal and happened so quickly. From discovering a mysterious lump in one breast in early August, to undergoing a double mastectomy in late August, to receiving an all clear report in September. WOW! A miracle had just occurred! Thank you, Lord! Now my focus could shift fully to healing.

Previous life experiences have shown me that healing is a process. It is full of ups and downs, twists and turns, expectations and disappointment. There is pain and relief, progress and delay. There are moments of peace as well as some exceptionally difficult moments. I do not know if I thought this experience would be any different. However, through this healing process, I discovered the 'sounds of cancer' which in turn are the sounds of healing like a fighter.

As a result of my cancer diagnosis and recovery, my husband assumed my driving responsibilities in addition to his own.

During my second week of recovery, in an effort to relieve my husband from the driving he had undertaken, I drove our eldest son to his high school which was 35 minutes away from our home. This was my first time driving since the surgery and I soon realized that I had attempted too much too soon. With each turn of the steering wheel, the pain I felt in my breasts increased, which seemed like sharp razors.

As I made my way home, I began to weep as I thought about the pain I was feeling and the entire process of losing my breasts to surgery because of cancer, which included the insertion of drain tubes to remove extra fluid away from the surgical sites. Sitting at a traffic light, I sat in that moment. I turned the steering wheel and my muscles contracted, my chest seemed to constrict further. The pain crept through my body as if I had been captured by a boa constrictor, who was slowly squeezing out my breath by wrapping itself fully around my weakened body.

The somber reality of those thoughts then led to thoughts about how much I was missing my daughter who was away at college, which in turn became thoughts of inadequacies in my roles at work, as a mom, and in my marriage. I felt overwhelmed with sadness, pain, and fatigue and questioned why this diagnosis happened to me. I questioned my purpose in life. I questioned everything.

While listening to the radio, in an effort to change the atmosphere, I switched the radio station and, almost as if on cue, my eldest daughter's favorite song came on. As I listened to the words, the tears flowed effortlessly. "I've been thinking too much. Help me!" were the lyrics the pop artist belted through my car's stereo.

Even though I was in bumper to bumper traffic surrounded by other parents, spouses, employees, and survivors who may have been facing similar challenges; I felt completely and utterly alone. "Help me" is what I wanted to scream out the window at my fellow commuters. Instead, I inched my car along allowing the tears to simply fall, weeping with no audience.

By the time I returned home my eyes were like the animated character, Garfield the Cat. Or better yet, my eyes looked like those of a heavyweight fighter who had just lost a round. They were nearly swollen shut from crying, wiping away tears, and more crying. "What in the world happened?" my husband exclaimed in shock as I entered the house. Without a word, I grabbed a pain killer, took a sip of water and turned towards the bedroom. Under the blankets I went, clearly in need of some rest.

The following days were full of nothing. I was committed to not making the same mistake of over-exertion I had made a few days prior and made it a point to remain in a low energy state.

Later that week, we went in for my follow-up appointment with the breast reconstruction doctor and I was looking forward to having my drain tubes removed. No such luck. My body had not yet fully begun to absorb the fluid produced by the surgery, therefore the tubes had to remain in place for at least another week (which became two more weeks).

The tubes had to be drained at least three times a day, carefully handled so as to not rip off skin at the insertion site, the blood and tissue syphoned and output recorded. Because of their locations, I was unable to turn on either side while sleeping or lie in a restful state. They were **literally** a pain in my side.

On our way home from the doctor's office, I was processing that the tubes were not removed, and in all honesty, felt a great deal of disappointment. While staring out the window, chin in hand, shoulders slumped, watching the world slowly pass by, I lifted my gaze a bit and saw Kennesaw Mountain in all its grandeur. I have always marveled at Kennesaw Mountain because of the beautiful views one can enjoy from the summit.

My cancer diagnosis and recovery are the mountains I am currently facing. At that moment I realized I could focus on how big the mountains are and how long it's going to take me to get to the top, or I could choose to enjoy the journey with my focus solely on the view at the top. These mountains served as a reminder of what God had already done in my life.

I was not ashamed of the tears I shed earlier that week or even the disappointment I felt a few moments before this realization.

Those were all very real feelings and a part of my process. They represented the sounds, for me, of cancer and healing. I was thankful for the reminder to focus on those things that are pure and noble. I was thankful that God met me right where I was. I chose to focus on the mountaintop and I will continue to heal like a fighter

CHAPTER TWELVE
Keeping It All Together

My husband and I are often asked, "How do you two do it? How exactly do you manage everything life throws at you and still manage to get everything done with such a large family?"

We attempt to keep life simple and have found the following tips have worked for our family.

1. **Empower the Kids -** We really encourage the kids to be as independent as possible and allow them to meet their own needs whenever possible. We have taught them to use a stool safely to get something to drink or grab a snack. We have taught them to make a few kid-friendly food items such as peanut butter and jelly sandwiches or Ramen noodles.

We also instill in them the importance of assisting each other as often as possible. Having this level of independence definitely helps when we are involved in other tasks.

Josiah enjoys cleaning the tables.

2. **Keep them Engaged** - The children are expected to help around the house. We tell them that we are a team and that we need to work together to keep the house maintained. From the youngest to the eldest, they all have roles. Josiah, our two-year-old, knows how to wipe off tables with paper towels, while Nina, age 4, assists with clearing the table, vacuuming, and putting away the silverware once it has been washed and dried.

Hannah, age 6, likes to vacuum as well and also helps put up dishes and wipes down the fridge and microwave. Joshua, our 9-year-old, cleans the stove, the countertops and helps wash the dishes. Azaan and Amali, our teens, when they are home, offer overall leadership for their younger siblings. Ultimately, the teens make certain everything is done before bedtime.

Additional responsibilities the kids have include: taking out the trash, making their own beds, and cleaning their bathrooms. Nina actually enjoys cleaning the toilet with the little toilet brush. Hannah cleans the bathroom countertops and floors while Joshua is responsible for the bathtub and the mirrors. Typically, my husband does most of the work and oversight of cleaning our home but keeping the kids engaged helps offload some of those routine activities.

Hannah J is busy cleaning off the fridge.

The boys are tackling the dishes.

Older sister Amali is adding some dramatic flair to "shutting down the kitchen."

LIVE EVERY MOMENT

Big brother Azaan offers tips to his younger siblings

Josiah is determined to showcase his sweeping skills.

3. **It's OK** - As a mother and as a woman, I sometimes have to tell myself "It's OK." It is OK if the floor is not perfectly cleaned or the kids' blankets on their beds are not absolutely taut. It is OK if the vacuum lines in the carpet are not perfectly straight.

   There are times, however, when it's not OK and at those times, it is important to articulate expectations and reinforce acceptable outcomes. With the kids involved in household tasks, there are, of course, varying levels of ability. Therefore, I have to be careful not to crush their efforts, "Hey kid, you suck at making your bed."

   That would be bad, very bad. So, sometimes it is simply OK and to instead say,

   "Good job! Thank you for helping out by doing your chores."

   The goal is a functioning household with happy well-adjusted kids versus a house focused on perfection. As long as the kids are trying to do their best, there is always room for grace. It is OK not to be perfect. It is also OK to recognize when you just need a break. A quick nap can make a world of difference!

4. **Have Fun** - Our family likes to have fun. Sometimes we put on music, "traveling music" as I call it, when we're doing chores. We let the kids let loose sometimes. For example, I recently learned my husband allows the kids to stand on one of our low coffee tables as a performance stage.

After my initial response of surprise, I reminded myself of my previous paragraph-it's OK! It is absolutely important for our kids to see balance: structure, and responsibilities coupled with fun and letting loose.

In every stage and in every moment, God has been there to guide me, allowing me to live every moment with grace. From dealing with abuse as a child and insecurities as an adult. To attempts at becoming a mother and not succeeding. To saying "until next time" to young adult children. To managing a large family with a special child. God has been there to help me to understand my worth, my self-confidence and my identity as a child of God. I don't always get it right and oftentimes have to seek His presence. One thing is for certain, His presence allows me to live every moment. His presence allows me to be a super extra ordinary mom. Invite Him in. You won't regret it.

CHAPTER THIRTEEN
Chuckles for the Soul

While playing UNO last night, Joshua looked at his cards in frustration after being skipped for the second time and said, "Man, I'm getting screwed over here!"

Me: "Joshua, I don't want to hear you use that word ever again!"

My husband, fully prepared to use this as a teaching moment asked, "Do you know what that word means?"

I braced myself...

Joshua: "It means when you take a hammer and a nail and screw it into something."

My husband: "Ok. We'll take that answer."

#Innocence. #ThankGoodness. #HeStillCantUseThatWord.

One night we were watching Michael Jackson's "Thriller" with the kids, and we got to the part where the zombies busted through the walls and the floorboards and Hannah shouted at the screen, "Y'all should have made that house out of bricks!"

Working with Joshua on his homework one night, I told him to look for the answer to his question in the second paragraph of the passage he was reading.

Joshua: "Is this the second paragraph?" He asked pointing to the third paragraph.

Me, in my terse Mommy voice: "Boy, you know where the second paragraph is!"

Nina: "Why did you call him 'Boy'? His name is Joshua!"

#SheFightsForEveryonesRights #NinaSophia

Breakfast table musings...

Admiring a desktop calendar a dear friend made for us, Joshua said, "Yesterday was October 1st. Hannah, your birthday is coming soon!"

Hannah: "Wow, we are almost at the end of this calendar. That means we are going to die."

I thought to myself, WHAT?!?

I guess I need to tell my friend to hurry up and make us a new calendar before this one runs out!

#TheseKids #Logic #TheEndIsNear

One day I was working with Hannah on her sight words...

Me: "Okay, the next word is NOT, n...o...t. Say it out loud and write it at the same time."

Hannah: (After a few tries), "It almost sounds like you are spelling SNOT."

Me: "Well, it would be if you placed an 'S' in front of the word."

Hannah: Erupts in uncontrollable high-pitched giggles.

#TheseKids #Lordhelpme

Me: "Sit still, Sweetie, so mommy can finish your hair."

Nina: "My name is Nina."

#ItsNotWhatYouAreCalledItsWhatYouAnswerTo
#WhereDidWeGetHerFrom? 😆😄
#NinaSophia

Joshua: "Mommy, I am going to eat spaghetti tonight and then if I am still hungry, I am going to eat some sewage and cornbread."

Me: "Sewage and corn bread? Do you mean cabbage?"

Joshua: "Oh yeah! Cabbage!"

#ICantMakeThisStuffUp

It's family night and we are preparing to watch a movie as a family.

My husband: "We are going to watch something a little different this evening. It is called 'Phantom of the Opera'. I know you enjoy musicals, Joshua, so this will be great!"

Joshua: "The only musical I know about is 'High School Musical'."

The incredulous look on my husband's face at that moment was priceless.

😂😂😂😂😂

Convo the other evening . . .

Hannah: "Mom, you look so young!"

Me: "Yeah, I was in college at that time."

Hannah: "Actually, you look like someone who came out of the woods."

Me: Mouth drops open . . . 😦

I had nothing to say after that! 😂😂😂

#Nomoremoviesforher #Kidssaythedarndestthings

On our way out the door for a family field trip this conversation can be heard:

Me: "You kids better fix some snacks before you end up looking like Starvin' Marvin!"

Kids: "Who is Starvin' Marvin?"

Me: "He's Boo Boo the Fool's cousin! Now get your snacks together!"

#GottaSchoolEm #ThemCousinsTho

Went to see a very good movie with my small people! We were at the part before the movie begins where the audience is told to be quiet and silence their phones. Nina turns towards me with her finger to her lips saying, "Shhh..." while Hannah leans over and whispers, "Mommy, did you put your phone on silent?"

#TheseKids

Sitting here enjoying breakfast of champions (Honey Smacks, of course) with Nina and Hannah. Everything was going well until Nina breaks out in song. Hannah then tells her "Nina! You're making me a headache!"

#ninasophiasings #headacheforhannah #siblingantics

Hannah's new thing...

Last week she overheard two people talking to each other in the store and she said as we were walking away, "Did they just say Justin? We have a Justin in my class!"

We are watching a movie right now and she exclaims, "Did they just say Sarah? I have a Sarah in my class!"

I think she's heard every classmate in her class over this past week. 😳 😆

The other night, as we prepared to enjoy cake and milk, Hannah asked...

"Does milk taste like cow?" 😂 🤣 😜

How many times can a remote controller survive a toss from a second-story loft?

#JosiahChronicles #SeventyTimesSeven
#BrokenButStillWorks #BungeeCordWanted 🤭🤭🤭

Hannah: "Mom, do you want to go for a run?"

Me: "Sure!"

Hannah: "Ok-Great! I'm going to be on my bike though."

#SheGotMe #ShortEndoftheStick
#MyRunninBuddy #WeGotThatMileInThough

Joshua: "Genesis, Exodus, Leviticus, Numbers, Deuteronomy..."

Hannah: "Who is Doo Doo Ronomee?"

Both burst out into uncontrollable giggles.

#ICan't

The new book bags have been placed by the door with care, in anticipation of a brand-new school year.

They are tucked all snuggled in their beds, Fast asleep with "first day" dreams floating in their heads.

New school clothes are laid out and hair is done, Lord, please don't let anyone call her "Dear Sweet One"!

#HernameisNinaSophia
#NinaSophiaGoestoSchool
#NinaSophia&PreK

ABOUT THE AUTHOR

Shatanese Reese is a trainer, coach and speaker on leadership development, diversity and inclusion. As CEO of Super Extra Ordinary Mom, LLC, she strives to help others find the extraordinary in everyday moments through riveting workshops, keynote speeches and webinars. Shatanese Reese is a certified Senior Professional in Human Resources with over twenty years of HR experience. Her career spans industries such as retail, banking and higher education and her training sessions have covered topics ranging from effective performance management, talent acquisition strategies, navigating employee relations matters as well as implementation of new HR-specific systems. Shatanese partners with managers and teams to ensure their greatest potential is reached through engaging and powerfully packed workshops. To learn more about Shatanese Reese and Super Extra Ordinary Mom, LLC, visit www.superextraordinarymom.com or email at shatanese@superextraordinarymom.com.

Other Books to Enjoy:
www.TheSolidFoundationGroup.com

Live Every Moment
by Shatanese Reese
Genre: Biography / Inspirational

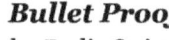

Bullet Proof
by Bodie Quinette
Genre: Biography / Inspirational

A Portrait of Virginia A. Smith
by Virginia A. Smith
Genre: Biography / Inspirational

Poetic Motifs' Significance of 9
by Kish Andes
Genre: Poetry

How To Fade Like Griffin
by Kendrick Henderson
Genre: Trade / Educational

The Pig Who Became President
By Alana Johnson
Genre: Children's

Set Free by Truth
By Amari Johnson
Genre: Children's

CheckMate
by Lex
Genre: Urban

The Cartel's Daughter Unedited
by Carmine
Genre: Urban

All are Available in Paperback or E-Book Formats
Anywhere Books Are Sold*

amazon   BARNES &NOBLE   Google Play   BAM! BOOKS-A-MILLION

* Your online review for any of the listed books will be greatly appreciated.

To learn more about the authors and/or their upcoming books |or| to obtain information about becoming an author yourself, please visit our website:

www.TheSolidFoundationGroup.com